New expat

THE ABCs OF PRAISE AND PRAYER
HOW 15 MINUTES WITH GOD CAN CHANGE YOUR DAY

BY BARBARA KOIS

Praise for ABCs of Praise and Prayer

Thank you! I have prayer books with scriptures, but I wanted . . . WORDS . . . to just be able to say throughout the day how much I love Him, how much I appreciate . . . Oh, my goodness, this is it! I needed help finding what I wanted to say, but you nailed it.

~ Amazon

I never before thought of all the wonderful ways we can think of God. This book is very inspiring.

~ S. Chery

Easy to read on a daily basis. Plan to read it every day whenever possible. A must read for someone with limited time.

~ Sonia Terrelonge

A must read of praise – When you are feeling down this is the book to read. It is short and concise and a quick pick you upper. If you need to just praise and pray, this is the book for you. ~ Kim E. Sturrup

This is an awesome book to start out your daily life. It is a great practice for kids who are just learning about God, using the alphabet to think of his goodness in our lives. It is also good for everyone who wants to know more about Christ.

~ Loretta H. Fields

A simple reminder that our relationship with God doesn't have to be complicated. A great way to start your day!
~ Amazon

Very well written and an unusual devotional book. Simple to read and insightful about the Bible.
~ Mary Cepparulo

Praise made easy. It's easy to read and understand. It takes praise and makes it a song to our Lord and Savior.
~ Cheryl Ann Johnson

This is the perfect book to pull out when you have a few minutes to yourself and you want to spend it with God. You would be surprised at all of the little moments that pop up that you can devote to praise and prayer.
~ Renee Stuck

Spiritual food – Great book gives you something to think about. Helps to open your mind to praise God for all His blessings to us.
~ Amazon

I thought the book was insightful on the various ways we can ponder on our Lord and spend quality time with him.
~ Amazon

ABCS OF PRAISE AND PRAYER: HOW 15 MINUTES WITH GOD CAN CHANGE YOUR DAY
by Barbara Kois

Published by Lighthouse Publishing of the Carolinas
2333 Barton Oaks Dr., Raleigh, NC, 27614

ISBN 978-1-938499-59-3
Copyright © 2013 by Barbara Kois

Available in print from your local bookstore, online, or from the publisher at:
www.lighthousepublishingofthecarolinas.com

Unless otherwise indicated, Scriptures are taken from the New Living Translation.

Scripture references marked ESV are taken from The ESV® Bible (The Holy Bible, English Standard Version®) copyright © 2001 by Crossway, a publishing ministry of Good News Publishers. ESV® Text Edition: 2011. The ESV® text has been reproduced in cooperation with and by permission of Good News Publishers. Unauthorized reproduction of this publication is prohibited. All rights reserved. Scripture references marked KJV are taken from the *King James Version* of the Bible. Scripture references marked NASB are taken from the New American Standard Bible, © Copyright 1960, 1962, 1963, 1968, 1971, 1972, 1973, 1975, 1977, 1995 by The Lockman Foundation. Used by permission. Scripture references marked NIV are taken from the *Holy Bible, New International Version*®. NIV® Copyright © 1973, 1978, 1984 by International Bible Society. Used by permission of Zondervan. All rights reserved. Scripture references marked NKJV are taken from the New King James Version. Copyright © 1982 by Thomas Nelson, Inc. Used by permission. All rights reserved.

All rights reserved. Non-commercial interests may reproduce portions of this book without the express written permission of Lighthouse Publishing of the Carolinas, provided the text does not exceed 500 words. When reproducing text from this book, include the following credit line: "ABCs of Praise and Prayer: How 15 minutes with God Can Change Your Day published by Barbara Kois Lighthouse Publishing of the Carolinas. Used by permission."

Library of Congress Cataloging-in-Publication Data
Kois, Barbara.
ABCs of Praise and Prayer: How 15 minutes with God Can Change Your Day / Barbara Kois 2nd ed.

Printed in the United States of America

Introduction

Just 15 minutes with God? That sounds like a stingy amount of time to devote to the Creator of the universe. But I've found that 15 minutes can lead to a prayerful attitude for the rest of the day when I start out this way.

This little exercise is not meant to trivialize our time with God or say that we can cram in a relationship with him in just a few minutes a day. Rather, it is meant to get us into a thankful frame of mind so we can look for God's involvement in all we do, in everyone we meet, and in every circumstance we encounter.

During my commute to work, I go through the alphabet and praise God through all the words I can think of about him that start with each letter. Verses that include some of the words come to mind, so I pray those to him.

When I get to Z and my 15 minutes is about up, I begin to pray for the things, people, and situations I care about and then I finish that and ask him, "Speak to me, Lord, and help me to listen and obey." I try to remain silent and listen.

The A to Z exercise allows me to praise God before I get started on all my requests and needs. It somehow helps me focus on God's greatness and his amazing love, mercy, and generosity to me. And usually that focus stays with me, at least to some extent, during the day.

I hope it helps you to focus on his goodness as you pray and listen for what he has to say to you. Add your own words as you go through the alphabet.

I've just added a new section for each letter to help you use the book for your devotions. Each letter now includes a story or thoughts focused on one of the words as well as a question or two to help you think about God and all He's done for you.

I hope these additions make your time with God even richer.

Please let me know your thoughts, suggestions and additional words you think of at barbarakois.com.

A

Lord, you are
  Awesome
  Almighty
  All-knowing
  All-powerful
  All-seeing
  Able
  Above all
  Amazing.

You are our Advocate
  Adonai
  Abba, Father
  The Author and finisher of our faith.

You have Adopted us as children.

You give us Abundant life.

> Now to Him who is able to do far more abundantly beyond all that we ask or think, according to the power that works within us, to Him be the glory in the church and in Christ Jesus to all generations forever and ever. Amen. (Eph. 3:20-21 NASB)

Lord, help us to Abide in you.

> Abide in Me, and I in you. As the branch cannot bear fruit of itself, unless it abides in   the vine, neither can you, unless you abide in Me. (John 15:4 NKJV)

Super powers

Think about God being all-knowing, all-powerful, and all-seeing. It's hard for us to imagine someone with that kind of amazing power.

We use the word *awesome* casually today when we like something or someone. But it really refers to something or someone who inspires an overwhelming feeling of reverence, admiration, or fear; causing or inducing awe, as the dictionary defines it. *Awesome* really doesn't indicate a delicious meal, a favorite TV show, or victory at a sporting event.

Our powerful God is awesome. He has no limitations. Nothing can be hidden from him. Nothing can defeat him. His plans will come to pass without a doubt.

I love the book of Job, especially when God speaks to him after all of his suffering and puts things in perspective.

"Where were you when I laid the foundation of the earth! . . . Have you ever in your life commanded the morning And caused the dawn to know its place; that it might take hold of the ends of the earth, And the wicked be shaken out of it?" (Job 38:4, 12 NASB)

And Job's beautiful answer: "I have heard of Thee by the hearing of the ear; But now my eye sees Thee" (Job 42:5 NASB).

If ever anyone ever accurately depicted the word *awesome*, it would be God.

What about you?

- What is it about God that, to you, makes him truly awesome—inspiring reverence and awe in you?

- Why not share that thought with someone today? You might inspire awe in that person too and help him or her draw closer to God.

B

Lord, you Built the Bridge between us and you and Jesus gave his life on it—the cross.

You are
>Beautiful
>Blessed
>The Bread of life.

You give us a Beacon of hope.

You help us Bear our Burdens.

You Blot out our sins.

You Bought us with a price.

You gave us the Bible.

To you, we are your Beloved.

The Battle is the Lord's, not ours.

You will come again for your Bride, the Body of Christ.

> Bless the LORD, O my soul, and all that is within me, bless His holy name.
> Bless the LORD, O my soul, and forget none of His benefits; Who pardons all your iniquities, Who heals all your diseases; Who redeems your life from the pit, Who crowns you with lovingkindness and

compassion; Who satisfies your years with good things, so that your youth is renewed like the eagle.
(Ps. 103:1-5 NASB)

Lord, help me to always Believe, even when I don't understand.

Immediately the boy's father cried out and said, "I do believe; help my unbelief."
(Mark 9:24 NASB)

Bridge building

Bridges are difficult, complicated, and expensive structures to build. Those who design them must be educated and qualified to do so because much is at stake where bridges are concerned.

The designers and engineers who build bridges must calculate all sorts of numbers and risks, like pounds per square inch that concrete and steel can support, how the bridge will stand up to wind, storms, and earthquakes, how it will bend or flex under pressure, and much more. Even the slightest error could result in the loss of life, not to mention property. They must count the cost not only of building the bridge, but also of having it fail.

Yet God built the bridge between himself and us and it is a very simple, seemingly un-engineered structure: the cross. But while the cross was simple and rough physically, like other bridges, it connects people; it helps them get to their destination. The destination, of course, is a relationship with God that includes eternal life, all because God built the bridge and our beloved Jesus was willing to give his life on it that we might live.

Jesus knew the cost: his agony, his death, his momentary separation from his Father. Yet he paid the price, our price, so that we could know God and live forever with him.

The most valuable and treasured bridge in history required Jesus' very life—so that we, by believing in him and receiving his precious gift—could connect with God for eternity.

What about you?

- Have you received the unfathomable gift of eternal life that Jesus gained for you on the cross? If not, receive it today and give your life to him.

- What about your relationships with others? Is there anyone with whom you need to rebuild or restore a bridge? Anyone you need to forgive or ask to forgive you?

C

Lord, you Care;
> You are Compassionate.
> You are the giver of Contentment.

You Carry us when we can no longer walk on our own.

You tell us to Cease striving and know that you are God (Ps. 46:10).

You can Change us, no matter how hard it can be to give up sin.

You are the
> Creator
> Comforter
> Counselor
> Coming king
> Conqueror
> Chief Cornerstone.

Jesus is the Christ.

He endured the Cross, despising the shame.

We can Cast all our Cares on you because you Care for us.

> Therefore humble yourselves under the mighty hand of God, that He may exalt you at the proper time,

> casting all your anxiety on Him, because He cares for you. (1 Peter 5:6-7 NASB)

Lord, help me to Call on you first, not after I have tried everything else.

> Then you will call upon Me and come and pray to Me, and I will listen to you. And you will seek Me and find Me, when you search for Me with all your heart. (Jer. 29:12-13 NASB)

Compassion for a canine

It was a sultry summer day when Sandra's neighbor called, asking if she and Walter had a new dog. Sandra said they didn't.

"Well, there has been one camping on your front porch for the past two or three days," the neighbor said.

Sandra and Walter's front door was never used because they and their guests drove to the back of the house and entered there. She went outside to investigate, walking from the back door around to the front porch, hoping not to frighten their guest.

The closer she got to the unsightly animal, the bigger the lump in her throat grew. Bleeding gashes sliced across his head. His eyes were almost swollen shut and running. Blisters dotted his mouth. He was so thin that his ribs showed. As she looked at the starved and bloody dog who looked like he was at least part German Shepherd, she thought, "*How* could anybody ever treat an animal this way?" Her heart pumped faster, and she cried, enraged at the obvious mistreatment. She felt an instant love for the wretched animal and, despite his filth and his wounds, she longed to cradle him in her arms and take care of him. He was black and gray and very dirty, like someone who had been through a fire. Sandra called him "Smoky."

The dog didn't move, but he kept his eyes fastened on her as she approached. When she got about three feet from him, he got up painfully and dragged himself away. With effort, he managed to stand up, and she saw that his back paw was hugely swollen and infected.

What a mess of a creature. Where did he come from and how far has he traveled? she wondered.

She tried in vain to coax the dog with food. Despite his obvious starvation, his hurt went far deeper than his hunger. She continued inching closer with portions of food in her hand, trying to gently persuade him that she just wanted to love and help him. He continued to drag himself away. The look in his eyes told her that he was not only starved for food, but also for love. Hoping that his hurt would be overcome by his hunger, she knelt to reassure him that she was not going to hurt him. But she could not convince him because his trust in humans was gone.

Sandra and Walter feared for his survival if he went much longer without food or water. They hesitated to pick him up and take him to a vet, unsure how he would react to their actions. It took two more days of gentle talk and coaxing before Smoky would let Sandra touch him and before he would eat.

Toward evening on the second day, Sandra went to his spot on the front porch to change his water, wondering if he would still be alive. As she approached, his tail twitched slightly. She again talked soothingly and approached slowly. This time he didn't drag himself away from her, but instead allowed her to pet him, opening the door for a happy relationship to grow between them. Smoky became a devoted friend and faithful watchdog that adored Sandra and Walter for his remaining eight years of life.

What about you?

- When has God showed compassion to you? Perhaps it was a time when you were at the end of your rope and he came through at just the right time. Thank him for all of his compassion toward you and your loved ones.

- Is there a person—or an animal—you could show compassion to today? Someone who really needs a touch of kindness or help?

D

Lord, you put good Desires in our us those desires! How wonderful is

You tell us to guard our hearts with all Diligence, for from them flow the springs of life (Prov. 4:23).

You are the Deliverer,
 Defender.

You Defeated Death.

You Dwell in us.

> For it is He who delivers you from the snare of the trapper and from the deadly pestilence. (Ps. 91:3 NASB)

Lord, I want to be your Disciple.

> If any man will come after me, let him deny himself, and take up his cross, and
> follow me. (Matt. 16:24 KJV)

Dreams come true

There's a story about a young man who told his friend of his dream of marrying a brunette, having three sons, and working as a teacher. The two friends went their separate ways and did not see or communicate with each other for more than ten years.

time, the young man with the dream married, ...en, and established his career.

... ran into his old friend at a sporting event, and the two greeted each other warmly.

"Tell me," the friend said, "I always remembered that your lifetime dream was to marry a brunette, have three sons, and work as a teacher. Did your dream come true?"

"Oh, yes, I achieved my dream, and more," the other replied. "My wife is a blonde, I have three lovely daughters, and I am an engineer."

"But that is far from your dream. Why do you say you achieved your dream when reality is so much different from what you wanted?"

The man smiled and answered, "God gave me a new dream, and then he fulfilled it for me. It is much better than the dream I had for my life."

What about you?

- What's the status of your dreams? Have they come true? Have they changed over the years? Has God given you things that, while they weren't your original intention, they turned out to be even better?

- Why not thank him for all the things he has done in your life that have brought you joy?

E

You are Excellent
    Eminent
    Everlasting
    Everywhere
    Eternal.

You are El-Elyon, the Lord Most High;
    El-Olam, the Everlasting God;
    El-Shaddai, the God who is sufficient.

You created the Earth and saw that it was good.

You have Equipped us with Everything we need.

If we wait upon you, you will renew our strength; we will mount up with wings as Eagles; we will run and not be weary; we will walk and not faint (from Isa. 40:31).

At Easter we say, "He is risen!"
    Our brothers and sisters respond, "He is risen indeed!"

> O LORD, our Lord, how excellent is thy name in all the earth! Who hast set thy glory above the heavens. (Ps. 8:1 KJV)

Lord, help me to be Eager, and not slow, to obey you.

> Walk in obedience to all I command you, that it may go well with you. (Jer. 7:23 NIV)

The right gear

You might be a camper or a hiker and you know the value of having the right equipment and supplies. Humans can only go without water for a short time, so water is a necessity when you're going out in the wilderness. If you don't have enough water, you need to be able to find it and then purify it by boiling it, as you may have seen on *Dual Survival* on TV.

We can go longer without food than water, but food or the way to get it is another necessity.

So when you're getting ready for a trip into the wilds, you carefully list, lay out, and pack up all your gear because you know how critical it is to have the needed items.

You have your knife, you have rope and food and as much water as you can carry. You have warm clothes and a hat to protect you from the cold and something to wrap around your head to protect you from the sun. You have kindling and newspaper to start a fire with. You have insect repellant and sunblock as well as your first aid kit. You load it all into your gigantic backpack and you are excited that you're just about ready to take off.

The moment has come and you pile everything into the car and head off into the wilds. You arrive at your destination, unload the gear and are pleased that you are able to hike five miles into the forest with your compass and other equipment.

It's time to set up for the night and you eat some more of your protein bars and nuts and fruit, drink from your water container, and find just the right spot for your tent. It has gotten unseasonably cold, so you're glad for that extra pair of socks in your backpack.

You will feel better when you have your fire going, so you look around for dead branches that are dry enough to burn and you pull out your kindling and newspapers to help you get it started.

Getting it started—you suddenly realize you have no lighter, fire starter, or even batteries and aluminum foil to use to get it going. Boy, this is going to be a cold night unless you can do that trick of rubbing two sticks back and forth real fast until you get a spark. What an item to forget!

Isn't it a relief to know that God didn't need a checklist when he was giving us all the equipment we need to live for him? He didn't forget a single thing we would need, even though at times we feel like we don't have the resources to handle a difficult situation. But in Philippians 4:19, the apostle Paul says, "But my God shall supply all your need according to his riches in glory by Christ Jesus" (KJV).

All my needs—thank you, God!

What about you?

- Think about a time when you had a need that you didn't know how you were going to meet and God came through—maybe at the last minute and in a way you didn't expect—to provide for you. Thank him for that and the many other times he has provided.

- Is there someone you could share that memory with? Someone who is waiting for God's provision and would be encouraged by your story?

F

Father!

You are
>   Faithful
>   Forever.

You give us our Faith in the First place
>   And the Fruit of the Spirit
>   And a Future and a hope.

You Forgive us.

You set us Free from our sins.

What a Friend we have in Jesus.

> But the Holy Spirit produces this kind of fruit in our lives: love, joy, peace, patience, kindness, goodness, faithfulness, gentleness, and self-control. (Gal. 5:22)

Lord, help me not to Fear, knowing that you are with me.

> Be strong and of good courage; do not be afraid, nor be dismayed, for the LORD your God *is* with you wherever you go. (Josh. 1:9 NKJV)

Fruitfulness

Sometimes I feel like I don't have the fruit of the Spirit—at least not all of it—when I know I shouldn't eat that dessert or play another round of a computer game when I have work to do. I don't feel like I have or am exercising the fruit of self-control.

And yet I know I have it because the Bible says that the Holy Spirit gives it to believers—*all* believers. He doesn't give some of us just love, joy, and peace and give others kindness, goodness, and faithfulness. He gives it all to each one of us.

When I ask God to help me be more disciplined, the thought always comes to my mind, *I already gave you self-control. It's up to you to use it.*

When I do use it, I have a wonderful feeling of accomplishment. Whenever we struggle to obey and then do so, we have the victory that is so invigorating. I'm grateful that I have what it takes to be loving, joyful, peaceful, patient (help!), kind, good, faithful, gentle, and yes, self-controlled.

What about you?

- Do you find one or more parts of the fruit of the Spirit to be especially difficult for you to display? Would it help you to write down and carry with you a note that reminds you that God has already given it to you and it's up to you to use it?

- Is there someone in your family, workplace, or circle of friends who especially demonstrates one of the parts of the fruit of the Spirit? Why not someone today you appreciate them?

G

You are God.

You are Good
>   Great
>   Grand
>   Glorious
>   Generous
>   Gracious
>   Gentle.

You are the Giver of all Good things.

You are the Good shepherd and our Guide.

> The heavens proclaim the glory of God. The skies display his craftsmanship. (Ps. 19:1)

Lord, help me to Grow in your Grace.

> Grow in the grace and knowledge of our Lord and Savior Jesus Christ.   To him be glory both now and forever! Amen. (2 Peter 3:18 NIV)

Showing God's generosity

One of the most interesting people I've ever met is my friend Linda. Right now, she lives in a retirement home in another state and has no money—literally. Her Social Security check goes for rent on the place and she has something like $80 a month to spend. The place even has bugs that they try to tell her are "lint" and some anonymous person harasses her by banging on her apartment door at 4:30 a.m. many mornings.

So I grieve for her situation. Let me tell you about her amazing life.

Linda earned her living cleaning houses. Until she reached the age for Medicare, she had no medical insurance. She had no paid sick days or holidays, no pension plan or IRA. Linda's mother died in childbirth and, as soon as Linda was old enough to understand the words, her father told her that she had killed her mother by being a "bad baby." Not surprisingly after a start in life like that, Linda has struggled with depression for many years.

I first knew Linda when she cleaned my house, back in the days of my material prosperity. We became friends, and she worked for me for ten years. Over the years, we talked and prayed together, sharing victories and heartbreaks. Both of us are mothers, and we prayed together for our children.

But financial reversals ended my luxury of Linda's household help, and ended my years of owning the house as well.

Our friendship remained strong, and we talked on the phone and visited each other occasionally.

During one particularly discouraging week for me, Linda called me.

"You sound down, Barb. Has something happened?"

"I didn't get the job I applied for, and I'm getting panicky about finances," I said.

"What a disappointment about the job. Let's meet for breakfast on Saturday. My treat," she said.

I was glad to see her Saturday morning, but I felt guilty that she had offered to pay for my breakfast. *If I had handled things better when I had money, I wouldn't be in this mess. Linda has so little, and yet she wants to take me out to breakfast*, I thought.

After we finished our meal, Linda pulled out an envelope with my name on it and handed it to me.

"I really want you to have this, Barb," she said.

"Oh, Linda, I couldn't take that from you. I just couldn't."

Her smile faded instantly, and she looked away from me, obviously hurt.

"You helped me years ago, Barb, and now I want to help you a little bit."

I knew immediately that the right thing to do was to put aside my pride and guilt and accept her gift.

"Thank you, Linda. I appreciate your help."

After Linda paid our bill, we hugged each other and parted. I was touched by her kindness. When I got home,

I opened Linda's envelope, expecting to find a $5 or $10 bill. Instead, she had given me $128 in cash.

Surprised and overwhelmed, I realized that she had given me a full two days' pay from her housecleaning work. *Just like the widow's two mites,* I thought (from Mark 12:42 NASB). *She has given out of her poverty, not out of her surplus. She gave me what she had to live on.*

Another lesson learned by example.

What about you?

- How could you show generosity to someone today? It may not be money you can share, but it could be doing an errand for someone or folding someone's laundry or cutting the grass. It will undoubtedly be very much appreciated.

- How has God been generous with you? Jot down five ways he has been generous in your life and in the lives of your loved ones.

H

You are High and lifted up.

You are Holy.

You are in Heaven and Here.

You are the Healer,
    Our Hiding place.

Thank you for the Holy Spirit,
    Our Helper.

You are my Hero.

You give us Hope!

> For you are my hiding place; you protect me from trouble. You surround me with songs of victory. (Ps. 32:7)

Please make my Heart and Hands clean before you, Lord.

> Create in me a clean heart, O God, And renew a steadfast spirit within me. (Ps. 51:10 NASB)

Lending a much-needed hand

I have a long, skinny driveway leading to my detached garage. In my attempt to be a "can do" sort of person, I patched an indentation in the driveway a couple of summers ago. It didn't completely level out the puddle spot, but it helped.

But one season that makes me feel anything but Can Do is winter and its accompanying snow. I love the four seasons; I don't think I could live in a place where the weather was one way all the time, even if were sunny and beautiful. Flowers in spring, roses in summer, golden maple leaves in the front yard in autumn, and those nickel-sized snowflakes floating lazily down in winter are all experiences I don't want to live without. I even enjoy raking leaves and cutting the grass.

The one chore I really find challenging—and one which I admit I avoid—is snow shoveling. Year before last we had several light snows during one week, and I just couldn't seem to get myself out there to take care of it. *It'll probably melt in a few days anyway*, I thought. Of course, it was January, and there was no reason to think the weather would warm up and melt the snow, but wishful thinking is one of my strengths.

Instead, the snow turned to ice, and horror of horrors, more snow fell, making a total of at least six inches on my driveway. When I realized the snow wasn't going to melt until spring, I tried without success to crank up my old snow blower. I got out the shovel and made a few lame swipes at the heavy stuff, finally deciding I could just gun the engine of my car the next morning and charge my way through the snow to get out.

Still more snow fell during the night and when I tried to accelerate my mini van backward and out of the driveway the next morning, I blasted myself right into a snow-covered flowerbed. The ice under the snow caused the car to slip off the driveway and into the yard, and I knew I was in trouble. I tried getting the car unstuck, but nothing worked.

Frustrated and in tears, I stomped around the car, and you won't believe what I did. I looked up at the sky and cried out to God, "Why do you hate me so much? Why did you let this happen?"

Can you believe it? I tried to blame him for my laziness! I guess I wanted him to just come down and shovel that long, slim driveway for me or send a gust of hot air to melt it all off. The silliness of my complaint hit me in a few minutes, and I apologized and went in the house to call my sister-in-law who came over with my teenage nephew and somehow shoveled and pushed the car out of the garden and into the street.

I thought of the Proverbs verse that says, "Go to the ant, O sluggard, observe her ways and be wise" (Proverbs 6:6 NASB), wondering what ants do when it snows.

After all that exertion I needed some hot cocoa and headed into the house for fortification before I tackled the rest of the driveway. I was drinking it at the kitchen table when I heard an unfamiliar sound out front. My friend Sue's husband, Neil, was clearing my driveway with his snowplow! Neither of them had any idea I was stuck—they live in another town—but they knew that I could probably use some help on a day like that.

What about you?

- Is there someone who could use a hand in your neighborhood or your family? A simple act of kindness can be a huge encouragement to someone struggling with a problem—or even a deep snow.

- Can you think of a time when God surprised you with a helping hand when you needed it?

I

Lord, you are Invincible
>Inimitable
>Imminent.

You are Immanuel, God with us.

You are the great I am.

You are Immutable—in this ever-changing world, how great it is to know that you stay the same.

You forgive us for our Iniquities.

Nothing is Impossible with you.

> God replied to Moses, "I Am Who I Am. Say this to the people of Israel: I Am has sent me to you." God also said to Moses, "Say this to the people of Israel: Yahweh, the God of your ancestors—the God of Abraham, the God of Isaac, and the God of Jacob—has sent me to you. This is my eternal name, my name to remember for all generations." (Ex. 3:14-15)

Lord, thank you for the Inheritance that is ours because we are your children.

> In Him also we have obtained an inheritance, being predestined according to the purpose of Him who works all things according to the counsel of His will. (Eph. 1:11 NKJV)

Impossible

Impossible is kind of a sad word, isn't it? "He's *impossible*." "My job is *impossible*." "It's *impossible* for me to get a job because I've been looking for so long." "My debts are *impossible*. I'll never be able to pay them off." "My marriage is *impossible*."

For us, difficulties can seem insurmountable—impossible. We don't see how we can dig ourselves out of a hole we've gotten into, whether by our own doing or not. We see no light at the end of the tunnel, even the headlights of an oncoming train. Life is glum and gloomy.

As Christians, can we just snap our fingers and our problems magically go away? You know better than that, and so do I. Problems are real and they are challenging and sometimes heartbreaking. They are stressful. They can make relationships difficult and they can affect our physical and mental health. Problems are real.

But our God, who owns the cattle on a thousand hills, who raised people from the dead, who restored sight to the blind, and who gave his very life to save us—our God can help and wants to. Nothing is impossible for him. Nothing is beyond his ability.

Jesus said, "And all things you ask in prayer, believing, you will receive" (Matt. 21:22 NASB).

For me, it's the "believing" part that is hard. But when I do it, God always comes through, maybe not in the way I expected, but he does respond to requests made in faith.

How about you?

- Is there something in your life that seems "impossible"? Something you have no idea how to solve or fix? Summon up all your faith and take the request to God, remembering that nothing is too difficult or impossible for him.

- Who could use an encouraging word from you today about something that seems impossible in his or her life? Will you approach, call, or email that person to share a bit of hope?

J

Jesus!

Jehovah

You are a Jewel.

Knowing you brings Joy!

You are Just.

You are the Judge.

You will establish Justice.

> The Lord longs to be gracious to you, and therefore He waits on high to have compassion on you. For the Lord is a God of justice. (Isa. 30:18 NASB)

Lord, may others see the Joy I have from knowing you so that they might be drawn to you.

> Now may the God of hope fill you with all joy and peace in believing, that you may abound in hope by the power of the Holy Spirit. (Rom. 15:13 NKJV)

A genuine jewel

The Hope Diamond, which is 45.52 carats and worth $350 million, is now housed in the Smithsonian Museum of Natural History in Washington, D.C. It would be considered a jewel by anyone's standards. Yet the Hope Diamond is not even the most valuable diamond in the world! It's the fourth most valuable.

The most valuable one is the Koh-I-Noor, which means *Mountain of Light* from Persian. It's a 105-carat diamond and its value cannot be estimated. It's considered priceless because a dollar figure cannot be assigned to it.

But even a 105-carat diamond pales in comparison to the One who is truly priceless, our great God.

In Proverbs 8:10-11, Wisdom exhorts us this way: "Choose my instruction instead of silver, knowledge rather than choice gold, for wisdom is more precious than rubies,
and nothing you desire can compare with her" (NIV).

Contrast that with what we read about the fall of the great city of Babylon in Revelation 18:16 "Woe! Woe to you, great city, dressed in fine linen, purple and scarlet, and glittering with gold, precious stones and pearls!" (NIV)

While riches and jewels can't save Babylon from destruction, those who choose God's wisdom have something much more precious than rubies and gold. They have the greatest of all jewels—Jesus.

What about you?

- What has great value to you? What would you consider priceless?

- Would you rather have wisdom or riches? Be honest as you answer this challenging question and talk to God about your response.

K

You are the King of Kings and Lord of Lords.

You are Kind.

You are the Keeper of our souls.

How great it is to Know you.

You Knew us when you Knit us together in our mothers' wombs (from Psalm 139).

Your Kingdom will last forever.

> How great are his signs, how powerful his wonders! His kingdom will last forever, his rule through all generations. (Dan. 4:3)

Lord, no matter what is going on in my life and in the world, help me remember that one day every Knee will bow to you and you will have the victory.

> As I live, says the LORD, Every knee shall bow to Me, And every tongue shall   confess to God. (Rom. 14:11 NKJV)

Kings and kingdoms

The song, "Something About That Name," includes a line that goes, "Kings and kingdoms will all pass away, but there's just something about that name." I love it that our God will rule forever.

He raises up kings and takes them down, but no one can destroy the kingdom of God.

When you look at history, nations and civilizations rise and fall. No ruler is so great that he or she is beyond the power of God.

The Bible gives us examples of kings who were both good and evil. King David loved God, despite his sin and mistakes. He was said to be a man after God's own heart. He loved God more than he loved his own power or wealth or armies. He confessed his sins and was humble before God.

What a great hope we have in knowing that one day, a truly righteous king will rule for all eternity—a King we can trust to do right.

Come quickly, Lord, Jesus!

What about you?

- It can be hard to pray for leaders we disagree with, but we are told in the Bible to pray for them. Will you take a minute today to pray for wisdom, courage, and righteousness for world leaders of today, asking that God would draw their hearts to him and that they would listen to and obey his voice?

L

Lord!
>   You are Love;
>   You are Light;
>   You are Living water.

You are the giver of Life.

You never Leave us nor forsake us.

You are the Lamb of God who takes away the sins of the world.

You Laugh at those who set themselves against you, thinking they can defeat you (from Psalm 2:1-4).

Your Word is a Lamp unto my feet and a Light unto my path.

> Jesus spoke to the people once more and said, "I am the light of the world. If you follow me, you won't have to walk in darkness, because you will have the light that leads to life." (John 8:12)

Lord, help me to follow wherever you Lead me.

   The LORD is my shepherd; I have all that I need. He lets me rest in green meadows;
   he leads me beside peaceful streams. He renews my strength. He guides me along right paths, bringing honor to his name. Even when I walk through the darkest valley,

I will not be afraid, for you are close beside me. Your rod and your staff protect and comfort me. (Ps. 23:1-4)

Love

The most talked-about subject throughout history, the word *love* has many meanings, some false. One dictionary states love's preferred meaning as "strong affection for or attachment or devotion to a person or persons." We rather like that definition, although an English professor defined love as "seeking the highest spiritual good for the beloved and acting accordingly." That one might be even better.

A search of amazon.com returns 375,970 books on the topic. Media portrayals of love range from heroic tales of sacrifice and courage (would that there were more of these) to prurient scenarios that debase both the doer and the observer.

The Bible mentions love more than 500 times, defining it more by its manifestation than by a description of the emotion. Jesus elevated the term to being the very proof of one's relationship with him when he said, "By this all men will know that you are My disciples, if you have love for one another" (John 13:35 NASB).

Often, we say the word, we feel the feeling, but we fail to put the words and feelings into observable actions. We're not always patient, kind, humble, appropriate, unselfish, unprovoked, forgiving, rejoicing with the truth and not with unrighteousness, forbearing, believing, hopeful, enduring and unfailing, as the "love" chapter, 1 Corinthians 13, characterizes love.

And yet we want to be. We want others to know we belong to Jesus because of the way our love shows itself to the world. We long to instill in our loved ones the sure and certain knowledge that we do indeed love them with more than words and gifts at Christmas and birthdays.

Yet with the busyness of life and the demands on our time, we may not love others in the way we want to, at least not consistently. In addition to our hectic pace as a reason, love has a cost—love costs energy, time, effort, comfort, vulnerability, the willingness to be hurt or rejected, and sometimes it costs money. And to top it all off, people can be hard to love, as we forget that we, too, can have our ugly moments.

Victor Hugo in *Les Miserables* said, "There are two things one can never do too much: pray and love."

We can work too much or worry too much or watch TV too much or talk on the phone too much. But we can't love too much.

Jesus showed us that with his life on earth and by his death on the cross. He was drawn to the poor, the sick, the broken, the sinners. As we try to follow in his steps, may we remember that love is a requirement of his followers.

What about you?

- Do you realize how very much Jesus loves you? And that he loves you on both your good days and your bad ones? Even when we sin, he still loves us, though he wants us to stop it.

- Is there someone in your life who could use a bit of love today? Why not take a minute right now and show that person some love with a kind word, a hug, a phone call, or an email?

M

You are Mighty
    Majestic
    Marvelous
    Magnificent
    Merciful
    Matchless.

You are the Maker of heaven and earth,
    The Mediator between God and man.

You do More than we could ask or think.

You comfort those who Mourn.

You are My God.

Jesus is the Messiah!

> All glory to him who alone is God, our Savior through Jesus Christ our Lord. All glory, majesty, power, and authority are his before all time, and in the present, and beyond all time! Amen. (Jude 1:25)

Lord, I am so, so grateful for your Mercy toward me.

    The Lord is merciful and gracious, slow to anger, and plenteous in mercy. (Ps. 103:8 KJV)

Mercy

One of the things I most appreciate about God is his mercy. It's beyond my human ability to understand how or why he would love such a fallen bunch as we humans. I mean, even the best of us is willful and stubborn, goes our own way, and disobeys his instructions day in and day out in large and small ways. I've known some admirable people, but the most admirable of them are humble and admit that they could never deserve or earn God's matchless love.

It's beyond my thinking as a mother to imagine God giving his only Son for us. I could never do that, but of course I'm not God.

And then even when we—I in this case—mess up over and over, he is faithful and just to forgive us our sins and cleanse us from all unrighteousness.

That's what I call *mercy*, what the dictionary defines as "compassionate or kindly forbearance shown toward an offender, an enemy, or other person in one's power; compassion, pity, or benevolence."

Thank you, my God, for your unfathomable mercy.

What about you?

- How do you feel about God's mercy? Do you know someone you don't think deserves mercy? How about talking to God about that person or persons and ask for his perspective on the situation?

- Is there a way you can show mercy to someone in your life?

N

You are Near.

You gave us Nature to enjoy.

You are Never too busy to listen to us.

Your Name is powerful.

You raise up and bring down Nations and rulers.

You provide for our Needs.

Nothing is too hard for you.

> And why worry about your clothing? Look at the lilies of the field and how they grow. They don't work or make their clothing, yet Solomon in all his glory was not dressed as beautifully as they are. And if God cares so wonderfully for wildflowers that are here today and thrown into the fire tomorrow, he will certainly care for you. Why do you have so little faith? (Matt. 6:28-30)

Lord, help me to Number my days and seek your wisdom.

So teach us to number our days, that we may apply our hearts unto wisdom. (Ps. 90:12 KJV)

Nature and the glory of God

The Bible says that the heavens declare the glory of God (Ps. 19:1 KJV) and that is so true, isn't it? When we are away from metropolitan areas with all their lights and we look up at the night sky, the scene is breathtaking. Especially when we think that God hung each star in place and named them. Psalm 147:4 (ESV) tells us, "He determines the number of the stars; he gives to all of them their names."

I love Psalm 8, which includes: "When I look at your heavens, the work of your fingers, the moon and the stars, which you have set in place, what is man that you are mindful of him, and the son of man that you care for him?" (ESV)

God named each star and how many billions of them are there? And yet he is mindful of each one of us. We have immense value to him.

Many of us feel close to God when we venture out into nature—the outdoors. We watch a mother bird carry, stick by stick, the materials to build her nest in which to house her young ones. We observe a tree, stretching its branches toward the sky, almost seeming to reach for him, its Creator. The enjoy the beauty of a flower that opens to display colors and fragrances that are impossible for man to capture except in photographs.

Or we might look up into the sky and realize that this same sky is overhead wherever our faraway loved ones might be in the world.

Nature—the canvas of the greatest Artist ever.

What about you?

- What in nature especially reminds you of God's glory?

- If it's possible for you, how about stepping outside right now and looking around you? No matter where you live, it's likely that you can see evidence of God's handiwork, even if it's just a bug or a bird or the sky overhead. Thank him for his glorious creation.

O

You are Omnipotent
  Omnipresent
  Omniscient
  Over all.

You Own the cattle on a thousand hills.

You are Our God.

You are the Alpha and the Omega, the beginning and the end.

You desire Our Obedience.

> "For My thoughts are not your thoughts, neither are your ways My ways," declares the Lord. "For as the heavens are higher than the earth, so are My ways higher than your ways, and my thoughts than your thoughts." (Isa. 55:8-9 NASB)

Open my mouth, Lord, to tell Others of your goodness.

How abundant are the good things that you have stored up for those who fear you,
  that you bestow in the sight of all, on those who take refuge in you. (Ps. 31:19 NIV)

Obedience

That's a tough one for me and maybe for all of us. I love God totally. I know that what he says to do in the Bible or through that quiet voice of his Spirit is for my good. And yet my rebellious streak rears its ugly head when I want to do something my way and not God's way.

I ask him to help me to listen to him and obey. I sing the song, "Trust and Obey."

And I think I've learned the hard way over the years that to ignore God's instruction is folly. It is harmful to me and others since he truly does know best.

So why can't I just quickly and easily submit when he prompts me to say something or to not say something? When I'm reminded to call someone I haven't talked to in a long time? When I feel like spending my money on something that might not be wise?

It's not that I never obey God. But what I need to do every day is apply 2 Corinthians 10:5, "We are destroying speculations and every lofty thing raised up against the knowledge of God, and we are taking every thought captive to the obedience of Christ" (NASB).

I need captive thoughts so I can do obedient actions.

Samuel said in 1 Samuel 15:22, "To obey is better than sacrifice" (NASB). God values our obedience.

God, help it to get easier for me to obey you—quickly, without hesitation, and every time.

What about you?

- Think of the last time God prompted you to do or not do something? Did you obey him? Whether you did or didn't, what was the result?

- What do you think might help you obey God more consistently? Scripture memory, on-the-spot prayer when making a decision, getting wise counsel? Write it down and review it next time you have a decision to make.

P

God, you are Powerful
    Pure
    Perfect.

You are our Provider,
    Protector.

You hear our Prayers.

You are the Prince of Peace.

You keep your Promises.

> And this same God who takes care of me will supply all your needs from his glorious riches, which have been given to us in Christ Jesus. (Phil. 4:19)

Lord, I want to Praise you.

> Bless the LORD, O my soul; And all that is within me, *bless* His holy name! Bless the LORD, O my soul, And forget not all His benefits: Who forgives all your iniquities, Who heals all your diseases, Who redeems your life from destruction, Who crowns you with lovingkindness and tender mercies, Who satisfies your mouth with good *things, So that* your youth is renewed like the eagle's. (Ps. 103:1-5 NKJV)

My provider

I had but one rosebush in the yard of my last house. I had planted it a year after we moved into the house. I gave the bush no care, and it disappeared. About five years later, during a time of difficulty, I felt too overwhelmed to do any yard work. My flowerbeds became jungles of weeds.

One day, as I walked up the driveway toward the mailbox, a flash of red on the left caught my eye. I walked over and sadly surveyed the overgrown beds, feeling helpless to do anything to improve them. As I bent to investigate, I discovered a lone red rose amidst the debris, a faithful remnant of the bush I had planted so long ago. It was as if God said, "I'm still here among the weeds and thorns of your life. I will surprise you with joys like this one along the way."

I can't describe how much the rose meant to me that day and ever since, as the little bush bloomed again and again. So when I put my beloved house on the market for financial reasons, one of the hardest things to leave was my rosebush. I knew that roses don't transplant well, and my thumb is not particularly green, anyway. I walked around the yard frequently, always winding up at the bush, crying and grieving my losses.

Amazingly, God brought a lovely and gracious couple from Jerusalem who bought my house, and I am happy that it is now theirs. But once the house was sold, I despaired.

One Saturday morning I prayed, "Where will I go, Lord? I've got three children and no place to go!"

I had looked at houses I could afford, and many were dismal. As I got up off my knees, the phone rang. It was a realtor friend who said he had a few houses to show me that afternoon. I dreaded looking at more depressing places.

But when we stepped into the cute, little white house near downtown, I said, "I want it." I didn't even go out to the yard or garage in my excitement over the meticulously maintained, charming home. The house had been on the market only three days, and we wrote a contract immediately.

A couple of weeks later, I had the opportunity to meet the owners. After I told them how I loved their house, the wife said, "I'll be working on the rosebushes in the yard this weekend. There are 13 of them." Tears crept from my eyes as I realized that God had replaced my one rosebush with many more. Surely, He surprises me continually.

Every time I cut a rose to bring inside and put in a vase, I am reminded of God's gift to me. Although he never promised that life would be a continual rose garden, he has shown me his love again and again in his generous provision for me.

What about you?

- Is there something you need right now that you wonder how you'll manage to get? Or have you given up on having enough money to provide for your family's necessities? Ask God to help you and then start watching the way he will meet your needs.

- Is there a time you can remember when you couldn't imagine how you would solve a problem or meet a need and God came through in an amazing way? Thank him for it today.

Q

You speak to us in the Quiet, small voice and lead us beside Quiet waters.

You are Quick to listen to us
    And Quick to forgive.

> He makes me lie down in green pastures; he leads me beside quiet waters. (Ps. 23:2 NASB)

Lord, help me to put on the armor of God every morning, so that I can Quench the fiery darts of the evil one.

> Wherefore take unto you the whole armour of God, that ye may be able to withstand in the evil day, and having done all, to stand. Stand therefore, having your loins girt about with truth, and having on the breastplate of righteousness; And your feet shod with the preparation of the gospel of peace; Above all, taking the shield of faith, wherewith ye shall be able to quench all the fiery darts of the wicked. (Eph. 6:13-16 KJV)

The quiet voice

Danielle has experienced the dreaded loss of her child. Her six-month-old son suffocated during his nap at a neighbor's house while Danielle tutored a student at her home.

Upon returning from the neighbor's house after the paramedics had tried unsuccessfully to revive her baby,

Danielle passed a bush containing a sparrows' nest. It was the first time in the years her family had lived in the house that birds had made a nest in the bush. As she passed, she saw a tiny baby sparrow lying dead on the ground.

She sensed God saying to her in his quiet, gentle way, "Do you see that little fallen sparrow? Just as surely as I am aware that this sparrow has died, I know what has befallen your little 'sparrow' today. Nothing has escaped my loving attention, and I am in control of the events of today and all your tomorrows. Be comforted by this sign."

Danielle knew then why the sparrows had taken up residence in the bush that spring. God had placed them there to comfort and reassure her precisely when she needed it most. No mother sparrow ever built another nest in that bush during the next fourteen years they lived in the house.

What about you?

- When did God comfort you with just a simple thought or a quiet nudge? You might want to write it down when that happens so that next time you're worried or troubled or sad, you can look back to how he comforted you in the past.

R

Lord, you are my Redeemer,
> my Refuge,
>> the Rock of my salvation.

You are the Ruler.

You are Royalty.

You Reign.

You Remove our sins far from us.

You are Righteous.

> Do not fear, for I have redeemed you; I have called you by name; you are Mine! When you pass through the waters, I will be with you; and through the rivers, they will not overflow you. (Isa. 43:1-2 NASB)

Lord, may I come boldly before you, knowing that what I ask in your will, I will Receive.

Ask and it will be given to you; seek and you will find; knock and the door will be opened to you. For everyone who asks receives; the one who seeks finds; and to the one who knocks, the door will be opened. Which of you, if your son asks for bread, will give him a stone? (Matt. 7:7-9 NIV)

A refuge and a rock

How comforting are these two concepts. We all need a refuge, don't we? A place we can go and be safe. The Bible contains many pictures of God as our refuge: he is our strong tower, our rock, and our fortress.

"For you have been my refuge, a strong tower against the foe" (Ps. 61:3 NIV).

"The Lord is my rock, my fortress and my deliverer; my God is my rock, in whom I take refuge, my shield and the horn of my salvation, my stronghold" (Ps. 18:2 NIV).

I love the lyrics of "He Hideth My Soul in the Cleft of the Rock" by Fanny Crosby.

> He hideth my soul in the cleft of the rock
> That shadows a dry, thirsty land;
> He hideth my life in the depths of His love
> And covers me there with His hand

That's what I need when I'm frantic, terrified, or just plain worried. I need God to cover me with his hand, calm me, and keep me safe. I take great comfort in knowing that he will do this for me and for my loved ones. And he'll do it for you and yours as well.

What about you?

- Where do you turn as a refuge in a time of trouble? Do you go first to God . . . or maybe to a habit or a person or a distraction like TV? Do any of these things satisfy you when you are in need of a calming, safe refuge?

- Why not arm yourself with a verse or a song that assures that God is your refuge and strength so that next time you are feeling panicky or upset, you can turn to our real refuge who will never let us down?

S

Our Savior!
　　Shelter

The Son of God,
　　Giver of Salvation

Holy Spirit

You are Sovereign;
　　Sure and certain;
　　Strong.

You are the Same, yesterday, today, and forever.

　　He who dwells in the shelter of the Most High will abide in the shadow of the　　Almighty. I will say to the LORD, "My refuge and my fortress, my God, in whom I trust!" (Ps. 91:1-3 NASB)

Lord, help me to be Salt and light in this dark world.

　　You are the salt of the earth. But if the salt loses its saltiness, how can it be made　　salty again? It is no longer good for anything, except to be thrown out and trampled　　underfoot. You are the light of the world. A town built on a hill cannot be hidden.　　(Matt. 5:13-14 NIV)

A dash of salt

My mother always put a dash of salt in desserts like apple pies to bring the flavor out. I'm sure many of our mothers did the same thing. You don't taste the salt but it makes the other ingredients simply delicious!

My son brought home from one of his adventures some Himalayan sea salt and everybody got a kick out of it—it was pink and seemed especially tasty. In fact, I'm giving my niece a jar of it this Christmas as a sort of joke/present.

Salt has been a valuable commodity for thousands of years. Long before canning, refrigeration, or preservatives, it was used to cure meat and other foods, making them last and not poison the eaters with rancid food.

The Bible says we are to be salt and light in this world and we must not lose our saltiness or we will have no effect. Salt loses its saltiness when diluted in water, so we must not allow the truth of God's Word to be diluted by the world and other belief systems that try to worm their way into our hearts.

In Matthew 5:13-14 above, Jesus exhorts us not to lose our saltiness so that we might share the light of the gospel and draw others to him.

What about you?

- Are you still salty so that you can represent the flavor of the gospel in your everyday interactions? Or has the world or political correctness or other belief systems begun to dilute the strength of your testimony for Jesus?

- What are the things, people, or activities that might need to be reconsidered so that you can remain steadfast and effective as you interact with others?

T

You are the Teacher,
  The Trier of men's hearts.

You are Trustworthy,
  True,
    Truth itself.

You are the strong Tower I can run to and be safe.

You will Triumph in the end and you Triumph now.

One day you will wipe away every Tear.

> But the LORD is the true God; He is the living God and the everlasting King. At His wrath the earth quakes, And the nations cannot endure His indignation. (Jer. 10:10 NASB)

Lord, help me to Trust you in every circumstance and situation.

> Trust in the LORD with all your heart, And lean not on your own understanding; In all your ways acknowledge Him, And He shall direct your paths. (Prov. 3:5-6 NKJV)

Trust

In Mark 9:20-24, the father of a boy who had been tormented by an evil spirit for years asked Jesus to help his son. Jesus told him, "All things are possible for one who believes."

Immediately the father of the child cried out and said, "I believe; help my unbelief!" (ESV)

Isn't that how we respond sometimes? I know I do. I truly believe God's promises, but then doubt seeps into my mind and heart, along with fear. *Will God really help me?*

God understands our human frailties, of course, and here Jesus helped the man who was honest enough to ask for help with his unbelief. We can do no less.

How about you?

- Think of a time when you asked God for help and then hesitated, wondering if he really would. Or you were sure of him and then doubt began to worm its way into your mind. What can you do to build your faith so that doubt will have to take a backseat to your sure and certain hope in him?

- Is there something you need to ask God's help for today? Are you unsure whether he will help you? Try responding as the boy's father did: "Lord, I believe; help my unbelief."

U

You are Up above
- Universal
- Unending
- Ubiquitous.

> Where can I go from your Spirit? Where can I flee from your presence? If I go up to the heavens, you are there; if I make my bed in the depths, you are there.
> (Ps. 139:7-8 NIV)

Lord, may I dwell with your people in Unity.

> Behold, how good and how pleasant *it is* For brethren to dwell together in unity! (Ps. 133:1 NKJV)

Everywhere, all the time

Ubiquitous is an interesting word. It describes something that seems to be everywhere, all the time.

Saying to someone, "Hi, how are you?" without the slightest expectation of learning or even caring how he or she is—is ubiquitous. We do it all the time and it is said to us constantly. But we know, and the other person knows, that we surely do not expect a true or accurate answer, such as, "My mother is terminally ill and we had to engage hospice over the weekend." Or "I don't know how I'm going to pay my bills because all of my resources and savings have run out and I haven't been able to get a job after two years of looking."

The ubiquitous answer, and the one we expect, is, "Fine. How are you?"

Advertisements are ubiquitous during TV and radio shows. They are constant and frequent.

These things can be annoying and shallow, but we see or hear them time and time again.

God, on the other hand, is ubiquitous in a wonderful way because he is truly everywhere, all the time. He's always with us. He is never far away and responds when we speak his name and call on him.

To me, that's pretty great.

What about you?

- Do you feel like God is always with you, always available when you call to him? If you don't, ask him to help you know that he is always there, just a breath away.

V

You are Very God of Very God from the Nicene Creed.

You are the Victor,
>   a Very present help in trouble,
>   of inestimable Value.

You are the Vine and we are the branches.

You will Vanquish your foes.

> God is our refuge and strength, a very present help in trouble. (Ps. 46:1 NASB)

Lord, please give me the Victory over temptation and fear.

The temptations in your life are no different from what others experience. And God is faithful. He will not allow the temptation to be more than you can stand. When you are tempted, he will show you a way out so that you can endure. (1 Cor. 10:13)

The vine

At the back of my tiny back yard are two very tall blue spruce trees, nearly forty feet tall. I can see these tall trees from the kitchen window and one summer I noticed that it looked like some vine, maybe even a grapevine, was climbing up the outside of one of the spruce trees. I paid little attention to it until it kept getting higher and higher in the tree and one day I noticed that some of the needles on the blue spruce were turning brown.

Now this got my attention.

I went out to investigate but I couldn't really get to the source of the vine because of the low-hanging spruce tree branches that went almost to the ground.

I cut away some of the growth and tried to clear away enough of an area so I could see what might be growing up the tree. I saw what looked like a small tree trunk at the back fence and as I traced it up, I could see it was the source of the vine that was now killing my beautiful blue tree.

Here was this thing that really grew up with no encouragement—it got no sun whatsoever, being covered by the tree and shaded by the fence. I never water or feed it or trim it. But just like other weeds, it seemed to survive on no care whatsoever. I often think that if my roses or other flowers I love could only be like the weeds, how wonderful it would be and what a beautiful garden I would have. I always equate weeds with sin that is so hard to permanently uproot and that just keeps coming back to bother us again and again.

I had to call in the heavy artillery, my nearly-grown sons, to help me clear away enough of the undergrowth and cut down the lower branches to get to the base of the vine. They love to use axes and stuff like that, so they made quick work of the task and then they attacked the trunk of the vine. This thing was probably six inches in diameter, but they hacked it down and pulled all the vines out of the blue spruce, which even in itself was quite a job.

Of course the vine has a meaning quite the opposite of sin in the Bible because Jesus is the Vine and we are the branches. Just like the branches of my grapevine couldn't continue to climb and flourish once they were severed from their source, we can't climb and flourish spiritually if we are not firmly connected to our Vine.

But there are both good vines and bad ones in the Bible. In Deuteronomy 32:32, Moses says of the disobedient Israelites, "For their vine is from the vine of Sodom, and from the fields of Gomorrah; their grapes are grapes of poison, their clusters, bitter. Their wine is the venom of serpents and the deadly poison of cobras."

Also, when Israel was disobedient, its vines were made to wither and be unfruitful as a punishment for sin and conversely, God made their vines fruitful when they were obedient.

I want to stay connected to the true Vine, not to some withered vine. And when I spot an evil one growing up in my life, my sin, I need to get out of denial, clear away the debris around it and expose it, remembering that my heavy artillery—the true Vine—will always help me when the job is too much for me.

What about you?

- Are there any weeds or debris that need to be cleared away in your life so that your connection to God can be solid and you can be fruitful for him?

You are the Wonderful Counselor, Prince of Peace.

You are Wise and you are Wisdom itself.

You are Worthy,
    Deserve our Worship.

You are the Way, the truth, and the life.

You gave us your Word.

> Great is the Lord! He is most worthy of praise! No one can measure his greatness. (Ps. 145:3)

Oh, Lord, I need Wisdom. Please give it to me.

> If any of you lacks wisdom, you should ask God, who gives generously to all without finding fault, and it will be given to you. (James 1:5 NIV)

The Word

The Word of God—what an amazing gift it is to us. Everything we need for faith and life is contained in its pages.

It has been compared to an owner's manual that gives you instructions on how to care for an appliance or a car. It gives us instructions on how to have a good life—not a life without challenge, pain, and difficulty—but in spite of those things, we can have a fruitful and joyful life by following its precepts.

Psalm 119:105 says, "Your word is a lamp to my feet and a light to my path" (NASB). If you've ever been lost in the darkness, this description has special meaning for you. When my children were small, their dad and I took them on a night hike hosted by our town's park district. We hiked through a marsh with a city employee pointing out interesting flora and fauna to us at dusk.

Somehow, and I still don't know how it happened, we got separated from the group and from our guide and found ourselves with three small children lost in the woods in the dark. We didn't panic, thinking we couldn't be that far from the others, but as time went by and the children asked when we would go home, I began to feel a bit of fear and even panic, as ridiculous as that may sound.

We kept walking but we heard no one nearby. We shouted but got no response.

Suddenly, as we rounded a curve, we saw a light and our guide said calmly, "Oh, there you are. I've been looking for you."

Relief swept over us as his light guided us back to the others.

That's God's Word—the light that shines in even the darkest times and guides us back to him.

What about you?

- When have you experienced God's Word as a light to your path? Maybe it was a time you were spiritually lost and a special passage spoke to you and drew you back to him.

- Jot that memory down and share it with someone else who might be trying to find the way in the dark.

X

You are eXtra good and eXtra kind.

We can praise you on the Xylophone (and other instruments)!

You don't need an X-ray to see into our hearts.

> For the Lord sees every heart and knows every plan and thought. If you seek him, you will find him. (1 Chron. 28:9)

Lord, make me an eXample of someone who has eXperienced your grace, mercy and forgiveness.

> I will sing unto the LORD, because he hath dealt bountifully with me. (Ps. 13:6 KJV)

Making music

I had so much fun thinking of ways we can praise God with the letter X. My son and I went for a walk near our house one day and we came up with words for each letter in the alphabet, using them to praise God along our way.

When we got to X, I told him that I had had to stretch things a bit to say that God is eXtra good and eXtra kind. He laughed and said, "Mom, that's an easy one. We can praise God by using a xylophone!"

Leave it to a kid to come up with the answer.

What about you?

- What is your favorite way to praise God? Do you like to sing or play an instrument or talk to him—or maybe a combination of all three?

- What praise song helps you express your love to God? Take a minute to hum or sing it to him right now.

Y

Yahweh!

You are You with a capital Y.

You are the same Yesterday and today and forever.

Your Yoke is easy and Your burden is light (from Matthew 11:28-30).

You say Yes when it's good for us.

> I am praying to you because I know you will answer, O God. Bend down and listen as I pray. (Ps. 17:6)

Align my prayers with your will, Lord, that I might receive Yes as an answer.

> For assuredly, I say to you, whoever says to this mountain, "Be removed and be cast into the sea," and does not doubt in his heart, but believes that those things he says will be done, he will have whatever he says. Therefore I say to you, whatever things you ask when you pray, believe that you receive them, and you will have them. (Mark 11:23-24 NKJV)

Unchanging God

In a world that is changing faster and faster with each new technological breakthrough, each conflict somewhere around the world, each new philosophy or leader or celebrity—how great it is to know that our Jesus is "the same yesterday and today and forever" (Heb. 13:8 ESV).

Companies and organizations change constantly—reorganizing, reprioritizing, reshifting so that we now even need a discipline called change management to help people change faster and faster and adjust to new situations.

Our health changes, our families change, our jobs change, our neighborhoods change, but God is the same; he is immutable. The dictionary says immutable means "not capable of or susceptible to change." Isn't that marvelous, really? We can count on him staying the same, even while everything else is on shifting sand.

We can count on one person in our lives never changing and that alone provides stability and security like nothing and no one else can.

What about you?

- Are you facing a difficult change today in your health, your job, your family? Will you take it to Jesus, remembering that his promises and his character will never, ever change, no matter what else does?

- Did someone come to your mind who is going through a difficult time of change? Could you do something to help comfort that person and point him or her to our immutable, unchanging God?

Z

You are the maker of the Zebra and all the animals in the Zoo.

You are Zealous for your holy name.

> Therefore this is what the Sovereign LORD says: I will now bring Jacob back from captivity and will have compassion on all the people of Israel, and I will be zealous for my holy name. (Ezek. 39:25 NIV)

Lord, thank you that from A to Z we can thank you, praise you, worship you, and love you.

> Now to Him who is able to do far more abundantly beyond all that we ask or think, according to the power that works within us, to Him *be* the glory in the church and in Christ Jesus to all generations forever and ever. Amen. (Eph. 3:20-21 NASB)

A lifestyle of praiZe

I took a little liberty with spelling here, but I wanted to end by encouraging you with the words of a great man of God, the late Bill Bright. At the end of the CD called "Praise [correctly spelled] and Worship" after the last song, "Our God Reigns," he said,

> When the Lord inhabits the priases of his people, the influence of the enemy is driven away. If our battle is not against flesh and blood but against the evil rulers

of the unseen world, then we need to use powerful spiritual weapons, and triumphant, overcoming praise is the most effective weapon at our disposal. Praise which results in constant victory is continuous praise. Praise that is a vocation, a way of life. Let's make it our regular practice to arm ourselves for spiritual conflict with a lifestyle of continuous praise.

I hope this little book helps you arm yourself with praise so that you can be victorious in your life. Thank you for praising and worshiping our great God and Savior with me through its pages.

God bless you.

Made in the USA
Middletown, DE
27 December 2018